Always
A
Blue
House

Always a Blue House

Lisa Rizzo

Saddle Road Press

Always a Blue House
© 2016 by Lisa Rizzo

Saddle Road Press
Hilo, Hawai'i
www.saddleroadpress.com

All rights reserved. No part of this book may be reproduced or transmitted in any form or by any means without written permission of the author.

Author photograph by Lori Rizzo-Cummings
Cover and book design by Don Mitchell

ISBN 978-0-9969074-4-6
Library of Congress Control Number: 2016949734

For my parents, Bill and Melba

Contents

BLUE ANGEL	9

I

MIGHTY RIVERS	13
AUTUMN	14
WASHING DISHES	15
OMEN	16
PILGRIM	17
MORNING	18
HIKE TO BOX CANYON, NEW MEXICO	19
INTERLOPERS	20
FIVE ZANZIBAR GIRLS	21
IN A PARIS APARTMENT	23
WEALTH	24
ARTEMIS	25
LESVOS	26
PRAIRIE EASTER	27
BERNINI'S DAPHNE	29
SPELUNKING, OREGON CAVES	30

II

THE COLLECTOR	33
JULIET AND ROMEO	35
MONDAY AUBADE	36
MEAT	37
MY FATHER'S HANDS	38
FOR THIS TIME BEING	39
WHAT DO YOU THINK ABOUT NOW?	40
DOUBLE DUTCH, 1963	42
MIDDLE SCHOOL	43

CUTTING	44
OLD CARS	45
TEMPERANCE	47
e AN ERASURE POEM	48
TRYING TO SPEAK SPANISH, TRUCHAS, NEW MEXICO	50

III

SNOW ANGEL	53
DECEMBER CHILD	54
REQUIEM	55
IN YOUR WINTER, MY FATHER	56
IN THE SHOWER	57
SUNDAY MORNING	58
VISITATION, A PANTOUM	59
LUMINOSITY	60
EVEN WHILE SNORKELING IN BALI	61
BEE SONG	62
STAR CORAL	63
TURKEY MEDICINE	64
DRAGONFLY	65
MERRY DANCERS	66
WHEN YOU RISE	68
SUNRISE WITH MOUNTAIN	69
NOTES	73
ACKNOWLEDGEMENTS	74
ABOUT LISA RIZZO	77

Blue Angel

— After the painting by Marc Chagall

Beside the open window,
she floats free, right hand over her heart.
Mouth open, an ecstatic sigh, she gazes.
Flowers burst open, deep indigo in their vase.

Her hair waves like a fish tail,
white wings like fins signal her advent.
A dress of water breaks from waves
sparkles into the blue, blue world.

In a dream-swim under three crescent moons
a house is floating or sinking or settling
into sediment on the sea floor.
It is a blue house; it is always a blue house.

She is my angel and no one else's.
I can keep her my secret or let her free
into the world. I don't care whether
she has flown in the window or out.

I

if I say blue sky
if I say bright morning light
will you follow me?

Mighty Rivers

Each day she
........cups her hands
....under the trickle
allotted her
........and dreams
....that her body floats,
hair spreading
........like seaweed,
....that the Mississippi or Ganges
pours through her.
........She does not want oblivion,
....but to swim
their cool ferocity
........and fill
....with silver purpose.
She craves
........Amazon
....rain drops
dimpling the surface
........as water returns
....to water. She wants
to ride Zambezi's currents
........between wide dappled banks,
....birds chattering
her processional.
........The thirst that rises in her
....might sweep her
headlong
........into maelstrom,
....force her into its rush.
She only has to dive.

Autumn

He said, *I'm moving to Berkeley.*
She said, *I guess I could live there.*
He said, *Why do you follow me everywhere?*

November poured down,
the taxi sped through city streets
filled with those words.

She twisted the wedding ring
around her finger.
What did it mean if not *follow*?

Later in their marriage bed,
he said, *I want a divorce.*
Promises like stones fell, one by one.

She thought about the taxi driver,
his eyes in the rearview mirror.
He would be home now,

hands cupping the whiskey
his wife would pour to ease the chill.
Sitting at the kitchen table,

he'd tell her about those young
people breaking
apart before his eyes.

Washing Dishes

White shards shattered,
scattered over the tile floor.
Another plate flew
past his head as if in a movie
just as she had often imagined.

A bird trapped in her cage,
approval was the worm
she craved. Not his half-
hidden glance as he turned away,
derision written in the curve of his lips.

But as she wiped that plate dry,
warm from its bath, porcelain
smooth, this time her hand
made the reply
she had never dared speak.

Omen

Hot sun pounded hot steel;
rolling over prairie,
car piled high with luggage
and pillows
and hope that this journey
would heal the old wound,

that she could set her face
forever in one direction,
stop looking over her shoulder
to see where she had been,
open her eyes
to where she was going.

Outside, heat shimmer rose
from bubbling asphalt.
When she stopped for gas,
her feet crunched
grasshoppers. She thought
of the plagues of Egypt.

Pilgrim

We followed the road
to Compostela,
searching for nothing more
than adventure.

Yellow arrows on signposts
pointed the way,
each fork in the road
a question with an answer.

This nonbeliever walking
an ancient pilgrimage trail —
irony lost on no one,
my purpose as muddy

as these spring fields
furrowed by the plow. The cross
at the crossroads made me uneasy
but not the old man

who stepped out into the rain
to help me find my way.
Even my faulty Spanish
could not impede his benevolence

which impelled me to walk on,
forced me to believe,
unwillingly, that benefit
may come despite ourselves.

Morning

Stopping on the side of a hill,
just after dawn and miles
already walked. We breathed deep
to make the final push

and in that moment,
sunlight shone through the trees,
mist curling its fingers
around spring-pale leaves.

If we had not begun our journey
when we did, if we had not stopped
to rest just then, we would have missed
that particular moment

when, on a country road winding
among nettles and buttercups,
witnessed only by cows and sheep,
we were washed in light.

Hike to Box Canyon, New Mexico

Golden aspen quakes,
blue sky shakes

with resonant light,
a white nimbus.

Canyon walls red
above the sagebrush.

I clap hands
and an explosion of wings

flies up around me.
Beside the singing river

wild possibilities
swoop and hover —

what I see and what
I have yet to recognize.

INTERLOPERS

Car tires stop.
Only insects buzz
in the flat-roofed acacia trees —
no human sounds.

Unbroken grassland
spreads out below me.
Serengeti. Maasai word:
Endless plain.

Across it, scores
of wildebeest
led by zebra scouts.

Heading north toward Kenya.

I think in borders,
human sealed
within such boundaries.

Thankful that, as yet,
no human fence guards
this animal migration.

I turn back.
They thunder on.

Five Zanzibar Girls

Bright birds, they settle,
        each head veiled,
                with dark blue wings
                        tucked around them.

Tropic sun blazes
        on turquoise sea,
                as they nibble and sip
                        after-school snacks.

One holds an orange cup,
        another a bowl
                as blue as a veil.

They stare out at ships:
        white tourist yachts
                soon to sail away,

and weather-beaten,
        sunburned Zanzibar boats
                unloaded by women,

vibrant scarves obscuring faces.
        Skirts dragged wet through sea water,
                their mothers and aunts,
                        heavy laden.

Perhaps the same ending
        lies in their five futures.
                But for now these girls
                        gather, unruffled —

   still confident
              in the possibility
                          of flight.

In a Paris Apartment

Loosed from ribbon,
peonies unfurl,
offer up silky aroma
as we drink in
evening light falling
gold across gold stone
outside our window.

Buying these peonies,
buds still tucked tight,
you astonish me
striding ahead into the shop,
fourteen years old,
ablaze with your first
time in Paris.

*I have decided
to stop denying
my love of pink,*
you declare as you cut
the stems, your deft
young hands full
of petaled promise.

Wealth

At home she sees kids on the street every day,
but here, the Eiffel Tower shining over her shoulder,

she can't pass their outstretched hands.
She asks for a euro, perhaps thinking it equals a quarter.

Tonight is too cold for someone to sleep hungry, she says,
dropping the coin into a waiting palm.

I am filled with the light of her
as she bends, dark hair swooping across her face.

Artemis

a leaf
I will float
down the river
through the green
green world
bend
my body
to the wild
under shadows
of tree canopy
lichen
mown grass
corn stalks
I will wear
tree frog
warbler
cedar
chartreuse aspen
just before fall
soft underside
of mallow leaves
pea shoot
spring leaf
sagebrush

Lesvos

That day I first saw Sappho's island,
Greek sun rose hot even at dawn's pale hour.
Scrub covered hills beyond

dust-caked car windows. I drove on,
clutch crabby and grumbling
like an old woman stumbling on gravel,

to the sea, past signs I couldn't read.
To the Aegean where the Poet
first spoke poems of love.

I should have brought verses to recite,
but my throat ran dry. Words flew away
like cinders, orange against sky.

Prairie Easter

Morning glory over the door, white star at its throat,
lavender-shaded like those Easter dresses
my sisters and I are wearing.
We squint into spring sunshine,
my hands on their shoulders;

stars flying through the afternoon sky,
stars I know are there
though no one else can see them.

Earth circles the sun. I feel it rotating,
its slow path circling down and around
like the morning glory sinking its deep roots
into Illinois soil.

My father, unseen but seeing,
snapping this picture so that my sisters and I
will always be here in our morning glory dresses,
always eleven and six and three,
pinned to the paper forever.

Stars wheeling in the afternoon sky —
      stars no one else can see —
keep me from flying off,
keep me here, feet planted in the grass,
in patent leather Mary Janes
with white socks just like my sisters' —
white socks that will trigger
the first battle with my father

next Easter when I am twelve
and begging for nylons.

But at this moment
I wear my Easter dress,
still his little girl
who hasn't begun to fight.

Bernini's Daphne

She is fleeing Apollo.
Arms flung skyward,
her body twists
from his grasp.

The sculptor has wrought marble
into white flesh rounded and supple.
Apollo's tight fingers dimple her rump
at the very moment
Daphne's feet grow roots,
her fingers bud leaves.

I know the story:
she ran from him over green swath
dotted with clover
until she stood wild and true,
free from others' hands.

I want, like Daphne,
to sink into that wildness.

Spelunking, Oregon Caves

I stumbled into a chamber, cool and moist,
marble glistening under rows of electric bulbs.
My steps rang on the metal walkways
above a trickling stream. Stalactites like long arms
reached for their twins rising from the floor.
Rangers warned against outstretched hands.
Human touch sours pure walls to yellow.

Just for a moment they flicked off the switch.
I gasped; I could no longer breathe,
buried in that pure black, as if my fire
had gone out. Then I heard water gurgling,
felt my heart beating. I listened
for what had not yet been unearthed.
What I could carry with me.

II

scalloped clouds floating
washed in opal twilight
we surely become pearls

The Collector

In a box my mother kept
an article clipped
from a small-town Texas newspaper,
yellowed and brittle,
its typeface out-of-date.
The grainy black and white photo
held my attention.
Reading the story was like walking
past a barking dog.

How my mother,
setting off for Chicago,
sold her car to a friend.
How late one night driving
that piney woods road,
black pressing
on the windshield,
her friend stopped
on railroad tracks.
Did she run out of gas? fall asleep?
All I know:
a train roared down
on that car at the crossing.

Everyone said
it was a miracle
she wasn't killed.
The train was splayed
off its tracks, the car crumpled
like a discarded candy wrapper.
An ambulance had already
taken her away,

but I always imagined her
inside the car
bleeding, unconscious.

And my mother,
she kept this warning
among valentines,
tissue-stuffed baby shoes,
an envelope cradling
my first cut curl.

Juliet and Romeo

That boy climbing a trellis to burrow
into her musky, unmade bed.
They're envied by those who can't see it —
those two had no sticking power, no grit.
Could never have made the long haul,
quarrels and tears — that part after "I do."
Marriage, rubbing of two sticks together,
would have proven too much for them,
hot house flowers twined in a bouquet.
Real life calls for the tough
and springy — dandelions or crab grass
in suburban backyard lawns —
those who come up fighting
after the mower has passed.

Monday Aubade

Four of us to get to school, four bowls of cereal or eggs,
Mother moves from table to stove, one need to the next.

Dad is long gone, his coffee drunk, his truck
driven off into pre-dawn darkness.

Monday, when beds are stripped of weekend,
school books gathered and sneakers lost, then found.

Sunrise peers over trees beyond the farm field,
birds chatter in the oak outside the kitchen window.

Four squabbles, milk spilled on the plastic tablecloth,
dog underfoot searching for scraps. Mother's face grim-set.

Soon the fat yellow bus arrives for my brother and me,
sisters make their way to school down the street.

The house falls hushed except for dog nails
clicking across the kitchen floor.

My mother watches the day come awake,
coffee cup nested in her hands,

gazes out at her garden. Then shakes herself
and clears the plates to set in soapy water.

MEAT

To my mother, beans meant the hard-scrabble poverty
of childhood: clapboard shack with floor boards set so wide
you could sweep life's debris right through them to settle in
the dirt below. Meat was a sign she had risen out
of that. Breakfast bacon so fatty it shriveled away to skinny
strips swimming in grease, grease saved in a jar on
the back of the stove, used to cook up more meat. Or pork
sausage bought in tubes, fried in rounds. Lunch from
Oscar Meyers: chopped ham, olive loaf, baloney fried
so it curled into its own little boat, her children afloat
alongside her. For dinner, hamburger: patties, meatloaf,
chili, in spaghetti sauce, with rice, but never ever cooked
outside on a grill. Outside meant bugs. Chicken she
bought whole to save money and dismembered into
strange pieces we never saw in a store. Thin pork chops
that came out of the cast iron skillet dried and tough.
Chipped beef from a jar, so salty it shriveled our tongues.
And oh, more dreaded even than gelatinous headcheese
or the chicken necks Mother gave us to gnaw — liver.
Slabs of black-red organ she had to smother in onions
and gravy to make us swallow. Meat. Cut or quality
didn't matter, just that it was animal we ate, proving
that we deserved to live in our suburban cracker-box house
identical to the others around us.

My Father's Hands

old, stiff fingered
pale and puffy, cracked landscape of use
nails yellow and creased, thick as hooves

left behind by his mother when he was three
pressed against orphanage walls
curled around emptiness

never played with his own children
never stroked or cradled them
only knew how to work

carried tool boxes, wielded hammers
gripped tiller handles, broke open Illinois clay
planted seeds to feed us all

now they flutter in his lap
moths beating against a closed window
clutching at air, at me

For This Time Being

The ache in his bones says
I'm still here,
although he can't remember
what he should do
or where he's going.

He still knows each day arrives
with night's passing.
That must count for something,
as he shuffles toward the end
he's stopped pretending isn't near.

I'm still here.

Until he falls or fails
to wake one morning,
he will rise and totter
outside to check for sun
or fog or rain or snow,
turn over one more day.

Forward or back,
he no longer notices.
For this time being,
he's an old man in thick glasses,
arms and legs shriveled,
eating chocolates.

I'm still here.

Inside, a small boy
reaching for the sweetness
of his mother's hand.

What Do You Think About Now?

Chicago. You knew every street,
every neighborhood.
Remember that time you drove
us down the Dan Ryan Expressway
in our 1968 maroon Buick Electra.
You pointed to the right:
The house where I lived with Aunt Ida.

Now what do you think about?
That small boy with wild curly hair?
Wide, elm-lined streets, trees leafing
in summer or standing winter-gaunt?
Riding streetcars to high school?

Do you remember me? Do you remember
showing me how to take the Illinois Central downtown?
The 1969 tickertape parade
after the astronauts came back from the moon?
Brookfield Zoo and Grant Park?
Those church group picnics I always hated?

I'd run those stupid three-legged races all over again,
or the one where you carry an egg in a spoon,
if only you'd say, *Remember, Lisa...*

Maybe if I took you there,
you would become yourself again.
Sitting in your wheelchair, you'll say,
There, we used to eat at Berghoff's
or look for Chock full o' Nuts.
We could buy a bag
of salty cashews and sit
watching Lake Michigan lap at the rocks.

If I went there now, every footfall
would sound like yours.
Out of the corner of my eye
I would glimpse you
driving your big car,
opera blaring on the radio.
I would know it's you.

Maybe I will. Maybe I will
cross those busy streets
and ride the El screeching on its tracks.
I'll turn and there you'll be.
Throwing my arms around you,
I'll say, *Dad, it's wonderful to have you back.*

Double Dutch, 1963

Pigtails flapped their black wings tied with small plastic
beads like bright gumballs. I watched those girls rise
from earth, their jump ropes dividing us. Not knowing
how to cross that line drawn long ago. Slapping blacktop,
their dirty Keds in need of white shoe polish, rubber soles
kicking up puffs of schoolyard dust. Their feet flew, left,
right, left, right, so quick I expected them to lift off
any moment like small jets. Pleated plaid skirts floated
in the breeze made by ropes that rose and fell in mirrored
arcs. The girls at both ends watched each other, brown
arms swinging round and round. First one leapt in, then
another, doing their two-step dance, eyes focused on
the far distance. They waited for the next arc, next swing,
bodies in tune with each other, feet in perfect rhythm.

Middle School

The bell
the dash
to the threshold
chattering
thirty-three bodies slouch in —

pants slung low
over two pairs of shorts
chipped nail polish
voluminous sweatshirts
covering bare-shouldered tops

eyes cast down
not cool to seem eager
better to mask the craving
that fills the air with musk

I could show them
to the heart of things
but a middle aged woman
in bifocal glasses
is far removed
they are sure
from the deep ache
of their lives

Cutting

-- for A.M.

The tool doesn't matter:
Needle
Pin
Paper clip
Razor blade.

Red wells from fresh
furrows
beside white-scarred
witnesses,
slashed
in taut young arms
hidden in jackets,
sleeves pulled over

nervous hands
that razored
needles, pins, paper clips,
blades
into her own flesh.

I am angry.
You have betrayed me.
Please take it away,
all that I can't bear.

Old Cars

How I longed,
at ten years old,
for the low-slung glamour
of a 1966 fishtail Cadillac.
Our neighbors' driveways
were filled with late models —
sleek convertibles,
turquoise or red
instead of our
'52 3-hole Buick,
with black body
bee-round and fat.

I spent my childhood
riding in back seats
of cars older than me,
great hulks of steel
from smoke-filled
Detroit assembly lines
parked in front of our house
for everyone to see.

Other fathers played
baseball or grilled hamburgers.
But my father spent Sundays
grease-covered, struggling
to keep those old cars
running one paycheck longer,
and when I waited
in the grocery parking lot
for my mother's return,
I hunkered down in the dust

of those rusty floor boards.
I prayed that no one could see me,
prayed to find a different road
to travel.

Temperance

To temper: to impart strength or toughness by heating and cooling

Life folds us over and over,
heat and cold makes new metal.

Moon's shadow side is blue,
sun side glows orange: I too

am halved. Let me learn the art
of going into fire, the journey

I must take to end the wary dance
begun in childhood, forge self

in sorrow's blaze, plunge headlong
into what I fear, become a spark dancing

to the sky. Before my bones mingle
with earth, may I temper into one.

e an Erasure Poem

Everything

        there   All   relationships

                    among them   inherent

    zero   to infinity

    simple patterns   easy for

anyone   but often

    impossible to establish   More

complicated

                              Yet all

implicit   when we begin

            amazing then

             guarded secrets

    should be wrested   by

means   not at all

natural

    Such a   one

                    cannot

be expressed

                until

                                a more intimate

connection   with

the story of this

Trying to Speak Spanish, Truchas, New Mexico

Ramón lays down his bundle of willow branches,
wipes his work-hardened hands on his khaki pants.

¿Hola, cómo está?
Bien.
¿Habla español?
Un poquito.

I listen as he explains to me *en español* how he
lived in Mexico *con su padre y sus hermanos.*

They grew maguey to make mescal until men
who sold *las drogas* came. *Entonces,* his father said,
"Go to *los Estados Unidos.*"

Ramón left Old for New, swimming upstream.
Truchas means trout. *Sí, sí,* I reply, understanding him.

In the field, a white horse grazes on spring grass.
Wind rises, tossing the heads of white lilacs at the fence.

Crickets sing. Water trickles in the irrigation ditch.
Snow covers *las moñtanas,* piercing the blue desert sky.

Ramón motions to the ditch, says something about *sequía.*
Dry, I think. He says *los indios* and 600 years, *la agua,*

points to the peaks, sweeps his hand down. I squint
into the distance, imagine *los indios* digging the dirt

to capture snowmelt. *Sí, sí,* I say to Ramón again. Only
this time it isn't true. *Adiós.* This is as far as I can follow.

III

words float hollow boned
settled for sleep, red birds wait
for morning's great O

Snow Angel

You must seize the freedom
of falling
backwards into powder.
It fluffs up around your face
and down into the collar of your coat.
Swish, swish — open and close
arms and legs padded
in your red snow suit.
Stare up at the winter sky.
Midwestern air pinches
your nostrils each time you breathe,
squeezes your chest.

Then for one moment
you leave the frozen ground.
Arms spread wide, you soar
over houses set down
in the prairie like Monopoly pieces
before you squeeze eyes shut
and settle back to earth.
When you scramble to your feet,
you leave behind your
angel skirt and wings,
glittering, white, blindingly perfect.

December Child

I was born under a December
sky, pale blue, the color
of skim milk back then
in 1956, the year I arrived.

A Texas sky with thin clouds,
mat of garden leavings
on the ground, mist rising
from pine trees in the woods

across the two-lane highway
in front of my grandparents'
four-square house, railroad
tracks stretching past.

In the hazy chill, roosters
crowed. Grammaw fried
sausage for biscuits and gravy
for Pappaw's breakfast.

They waited, hands wrapped
tight around coffee cups,
silent, impatient
for the first grandchild

to be born to them
there in East Texas,
not knowing she would also be
the first one to leave.

Requiem

Sapling,
heartwood laid bare,
quivering, snapped
by vandal hands. Sap
oozing from its warm center,
unable to flow, limbs
torn, bark rent, cold
on the ground.
I sing this to you and all
the lost trees of my life.
Backyard cherry and apple,
my childhood blooming
pink without me.
Spreading elm slowly
shriveling, wasted by disease.
Then every tree in the woods
behind my school,
chainsaws ripping the air,
moan of trunks cleaved
and crashing, sunlight
suddenly sharp
without leaf dapple.
All are gone.
These hands are empty,
bereft of leaves.

In Your Winter, My Father

memories float like seeds
through the air

blown from trees
winter-bared

mingle with others
in the damp loam

split wide open
in this dark place

your mind's tangled roots
create stories

we do not know
we who have known you

all our lives
slip slowly from you

as you remake us
into forms we have never been

In the Shower

Water beating
Monday-bruised body,
I'm struck by this double offering:
Clarifying Face Wash, Clarifying Shampoo,
their promises wreathed
in leaves printed on plastic.
What clarity
could I hope to gain?

If I were a praying woman
I might chant,
swirling circles on my scalp,
as suds rise toward heaven.
Still unclear, I seek another baptism.
Eyelids and lips closed,
my hands anoint my face.

I have watched men wash
before entering a mosque to pray.
Maybe that gave them
a straight path to God —
mystery I can't shed light on
even with my head
cleared for strong thinking.

I step from the shower,
hair and skin shining
like a gold-leafed icon.
Still lacking illumination,
I muddle myself into a towel.

Sunday Morning

Each Sunday you sit
among others, heads bobbing
in wheelchairs, as a minister
volunteers prayer and hymns.
You can still sing every word.

I wonder if you think about God.
Does faith remain
when memory is lost?
At least you have forgotten
your anger at my unbelief.

You fold into yourself, dying
day by day, heart failing,
legs and feet puffy,
shuffling your wheelchair
down the hall of your final home.

Opening an envelope,
your hands shake
so I finally take it from you.
You are puzzled by a picture
of ocean waves: *What's that?*

Too late now to ask
how you wish to be laid to rest.
I buried my cat under an apple tree.
Father, if I could,
I'd do the same for you.

Visitation, a Pantoum

rosary of black pearls
twenty-four pelicans
head north along the coast
wings spread wide

twenty-four pelicans
stitch sky and waves together
wings spread wide
low over water

stitch sky and waves together
singing a blue prayer
low over water
slip through fog

singing a blue prayer
head north along the coast
slip through fog
rosary of black pearls

Luminosity

For the Bioluminescent Bay, Vieques, Puerto Rico.

We slide silently
through ripples
reflecting
the approaching moon.
A glitter of green
lights the bay.

Radiance glazes
my fingertips
as I dip
into the water,
raising my hands
to sprinkle stars.

Twilight clasps us
in humid embrace.
Mosquitos hum
as distant birds
declare their intention
to settle feathers
into night nests.

Our kayaks bob
and nudge each other,
as one by one
we slip in
to swim through light.
We float in our
luminous bodies,
reluctant to return.

Even While Snorkeling in Bali

I float through blue waters, breath steady
in the tube. And here you are beside me.

I remember how you loved swimming.
How each summer you would strike far out

into Lake Michigan — Mother standing on the shore,
hand shading her eyes, afraid.

But you were never afraid. You swam true,
far out into pale water. Then, flipping over,

you floated long minutes before heading
back to shore. And I, once again, have slipped

from a boat into the sea. Coral waves and fish
dart past my mask, their bright stripes flashing

in the sunlight refracted through clear water.
Oh Father, how you would have loved this.

Bee Song

we sisters
visit one sticky
yellow center
then the next
nestle our striped
fuzzy bodies inside

search for sweet
syrupy beads
rolling in pollen
till we clothe our legs
in gold
we sigh and hum

come sing with us
raise your face to light
soak in nectar ecstasy
mingle your hands
in blossoms
crabapple spring

Star Coral

white dome
with petal-shaped dimples
as if flowers
fell to the bottom
of the ocean
and kissed this coral

as if it broke free
and rode
up to shore
joining other wanderers
leaving their bones
so sea creatures
might find a home

until this human
interloper came
wishing she were innocent
but greedy really
to take this treasure
far from where it belongs
turned it into flotsam
lying lightly in her palm

Turkey Medicine

Flock of wild turkeys tiptoe
from the shade of oak trees.
Sun blisters the summer sky.
I laze under the pergola,
watching two hens with half-grown
chicks peck at bugs in the grass.
Feathers sleek under noon light,
they place their feet with care,
necks bobbing in tandem.
Some say turkey medicine
is creating harmony, sharing gifts.
What gifts do I give?
Easier to sit back and watch.
They graze their way back
into tree shadow, disappear
like smoke, leave me
one perfect wing feather.

Dragonfly

I am the iridescent,
four-winged messenger,
lingering along
grass stem's edge,
balanced by
my needle tail.

Don't be fooled
as I flit and hover —
my free flight's
an illusion. I am hunting,
faceted eyes
scanning the reeds.

Glistening in the sun,
my wings' webs
carry words
that spill into stillness
between rest and effort.

Don't worry about
what will come.
Only watch
and remember:
flowers open wide.

Merry Dancers

My sixth grade year I discovered
aurora borealis. Plagiarizing my way
through encyclopedias, I slipped
my report's pages into a green folder.

In Finland they believed a magic fox
swept his tail through the night,
scattering snow to ignite
the sky, bright above silent forests.

Resin rose pungent from dark pines
under that mythic fox fire:
revontulet.
I wanted those lights for my own,

flickering like ghosts in deep winter,
better than Christmas bulbs strung
across front porches I passed
on my way home from school.

My own Midwestern sky was a simple
black, dotted only with stars or clouds
no matter how far back I tipped my head.
Until one night, my parents —

like Freyja and Óðr leaping
from their cat-pulled chariot,
my brother in tow, a small sprite
in his Cub Scout blue —

rushed in to sweep me into icy air.
There we watched aurora's merry dancers
in their shimmering dresses,
emerald, violet and azure.

When You Rise

You are stone bleached pale,
tumbled in sand until smooth.

You are ash and bone, stirred
into soil under crabapple tree

beneath a window cracked
wide from summer song.

Bloom white, quiver along a branch
sharp edged. Trace your own form,

driftwood-self drawing toward shore,
onto a beach blessed by waves.

Abide in the light until a warbler's
cry fills the timbal-clouded sky.

Surrender yourself to air.

SUNRISE WITH MOUNTAIN

"Hollyhock With Pedernal" by Georgia O'Keeffe, 1937

Hollyhock's petals
fill with dew;
great pinwheels
pink and white.
This is the time
before they wilt
in the bone-dry
midday heat.

Pluck one to tuck
behind my ear,
its scent grazing
my cheek.
Pluck another to hold
high against
now barely-blue sky,
fragile yellow sun
nestled
in the middle.

Wrap the shawl
of morning
around my shoulders,
as the green valley
enfolds Pedernal.

Soon I will rise
to the day's work.
Soon shadows
will fade
from the mountain,
rocks will glow red.

Notes

—Luminosity:

bioluminescence is caused by dinoflagellates, oceanic plankton that glow blue and green when water is agitated.

—*e*, an Erasure Poem:

this is a form of "found" poetry, made by deleting words or sections from a text, and arranging what remains as poetry. The initial text for this poem was taken from page 154 of *What Makes Numbers Interesting* by Constance Reid (A.K Peters/CRC Press, 2006).

—Merry Dancers:

Norwegians called the aurora borealis "merry dancers"
Finnish: *revontulet* means fox fire
Freyja and Óðr, Norse goddess and her husband.

—Sunrise With Mountain:

Pedernal is a mountain in New Mexico painted many times by Georgia O'Keeffe.

Acknowledgements

First and foremost, I want to thank Ruth Thompson and Don Mitchell of Saddle Road Press for their belief in my work. It was a pleasure to work with such a supportive editor and designer.

I am forever indebted to my Flamingos: Barbara Yoder, Michelle Wing, Ruth Thompson, Barbara Rockman, Tania Pryputniewicz, Marcia Meier, Sandra Hunter and Jayne Benjulian. These wonderful women writers have given me encouragement and advice as well as laughter and good food. I couldn't have completed this collection without them.

To the women of AROHO, including Martha Andrews Donovan, Maura MacNeil and Marlene Samuels, I will never forget our time in the desert.

Without Charlotte Muse, my first and most important poetry teacher, I would never have become the poet I am.

I'd also like to thank my circle of friends too numerous to list here for their love and support, and for always keeping me on my toes. I'm still astonished by how wide my circle has grown. You know who you are.

Finally, my deepest gratitude for my family: my parents Bill and Melba who taught me the satisfaction of hard work; siblings Paul, Lori and Lana who have given me lots of rough and tumble through the years; siblings-in-law John, Barb and Jill who have added zest to our family; and last but never least, my niece Felicity who has given more light to my life than I ever imagined possible.

Thanks to the following journals, prizes and anthologies, in which these poems appeared, often in different forms or with different titles.

"Serengeti Afternoon" won first prize in the 2011 Bay Area Poets Coalition Maggie H. Meyer Poetry Contest.

"Sunrise With Mountain" won second prize in the 2011 Bay Area Poets Coalition Maggie H. Meyer Poetry Contest.

"Sunrise With Mountain," "Hike to Box Canyon, New Mexico," "In a Paris Apartment," "December Child," and "Five Zanzibar Girls" appeared in *Aspiring to Inspire Anthology* (Durham Editing and E-Books).

"Star Coral" and "Bee Song" appeared in *Sugar Mule Literary Magazine's Women Writing Nature Anthology*.

"Pilgrim" appeared in *RiverLit Journal*.

"Morning," "Interlopers," and "Serengeti Afternoon" appeared in *DoveTales "Nature" An International Journal of the Arts Published by Writing for Peace* (May 2015).

"Interlopers," "Serengeti Afternoon," "Dragonfly," and "Bernini's Daphne" appeared in *When Women Waken Nature Issue*.

"Lesvos" and "Washing Dishes" appeared in *When Women Waken Being Issue*.

"Old Cars" and "Prairie Easter" appeared in *Allegro Poetry Journal*.

"Autumn" appeared in *Naugatuck River Review*.

"Double Dutch" appeared in *Rabbit 19*.

About Lisa Rizzo

Lisa Rizzo is the author of *In the Poem an Ocean* (Big Table Publishing, 2011). Her work has also appeared in a variety of journals and anthologies such as *Calyx Journal, 13th Moon,* and *DoveTales "Nature" An International Journal of the Arts* (Writing for Peace, May 2015). Two of her poems received 1st and 2nd prizes in the 2011 Maggi H. Meyer Poetry Prize competition.

She blogs at Poet Teacher Seeks World and can be reached at www.lisarizzopoetry.com.

Lisa manages to combine her love of words and poetry with her day job. She spent 23 years as a middle school English/Language Arts teacher. Now she works as an instructional coach, helping teachers improve their reading and writing instruction.

Born in Texas, Lisa grew up in Chicago and moved to the San Francisco Bay Area 36 years ago. Even though she has almost settled down, she still travels as often as she can.

www.ingramcontent.com/pod-product-compliance
Lightning Source LLC
Chambersburg PA
CBHW022228010526
44113CB00033B/769